BREATHING SPACE

BREATHING SPACE

CLARE BRANT

Shoestring Press

Printed by imprintdigital
Upton Pyne, Exeter
www.digital.imprint.co.uk

Typesetting and cover design by narrator
www.narrator.me.uk
info@narrator.me.uk
033 022 300 39

Published by Shoestring Press
19 Devonshire Avenue, Beeston, Nottingham, NG9 1BS
(0115) 925 1827
www.shoestringpress.co.uk

First published 2020

ISBN 978-1-912524-55-6

ACKNOWLEDGEMENTS

My thanks to everyone who contributed in various ways to these poems, especially to John Lucas, generous editor and poetry champion, and to Ruth O'Callaghan, fine poet, for unerring suggestions. Special thanks to Roger Perkins, whose sculptural installation *There's a Red House Over Yonder* (2019) provided specific inspirations and whose request for poems to accompany his brilliant work led to ones marked § in the text, which take ideas of home as their subject. Motifs of home spill into other poems too. You can see more of the exhibition via the hemingwayart website (see below). Thanks to Max Saunders for encouraging poems inspired by the paintings of Alfred Cohen, and to Nicola Watson for inviting me to participate in *Romantic Europe: The Virtual Exhibition* (RÊVE; see website below). Thanks also to Katherine Armstrong, Bridget Lubbock, Eric Larson, Claire Cox and Teresa Bruś for tuning in, and to my family, especially Chris and Sarah Brant, for their support.

Websites:

https://www.hemingwayart.co.uk/artists/curated-by/roger-perkins---sculpture

http://www.euromanticism.org/virtual-exhibition/

CONTENTS

ABODE, SANCTUARY, LIGHT §

Home is where you need no door
where all doors open
all windows let in light

shelter, sustenance and warmth
where staging of repair finds air
where coats peg being's outer bunting

watching place and listening post
power pack and plug
burrow, web and nest.

ALARMED

WPC was on the doorstep
only one
if there's really bad news
they send two

there's been a burglary a few doors down
nobody's hurt, some jewellery is gone

not to worry but make sure you lock your doors and windows
check outside areas, hide tools away
and keep your eyes peeled
take care, goodbye

I shut the door,
leaflet in hand
keep all valuables out of sight, it urges me
even sight of WPC.

ALFRED COHEN SEASCAPE

'these colours render a mood difficult to forget' – Josef Herman, RA

Out to sea there's a boat
   steaming purposefully
      against the waves

wind and sea are friends today
   gleefully
      the sea is seaglass green

of all the many tubes to choose
   viridian
      crested with white

as shore-side roofs applaud
   with an echo
      the ship's funnel blows back

we're going somewhere
   we're rooted to the spot
      stirred by the wind

out of doors
   out of reach
      it's crazy and serene.

ALL IN ONE

Tonight I am omniscient
in ways I had no idea were thinkable

until omnipotence
descended

while larks and I
ascended

glint of an unnamed star
deep at the limits of what's possible

seen from afar.

AMPHIBIAN DEPLETION

Toadspawn comes in necklaces
frogspawn falls in shawls
newts bind their single eggs to leaves

frog mothers size up ponds and unchoked streams
dampness is all
amphibian chronicles lace new descendants
in carpet page of dappled shade

they wriggle in their mirror water
sure in their genes, birth-righted
disappearing frog-populated dream.

BALLADRY

Slave of thresholds I am trodden on like a carpet
as yellow tulip waterless
I bow down, courtier
to the emperor of grief

distance, deceptions, illusions, memories
flash in the valley
the journey is long
we are not young

engine on turntable waits for its swivel
night's warming up ballads
my fair love, my sweet love, my true love
we know how it ends.

BARN OWL TRACE

Being rotten is productive here
the trees have coats of moss and the stumps
have frills of fungi
the ground is soft from years of leaf mould
packing down, springy with flights of oak leaves
that ghost the winter surface

nothing moves
or not that you can see
you'd think it a dead place
or a silence, motionless
unless you'd seen beside one stump
a pellet

matted, mouse-coloured, not aromatic
except to the dog's keen nose as pomander to cardinal
we examine it for clues of mouse
small bones, fur, whatever escaped digestion
whatever was joining the flow of rot
and decomposing whatever was.

BETTER IMPERMANENCE THAN FINALITY §

They marvel at
how filigree can bear the weight
of dreams, of home

structure and outline interlock
the home you dreamt of as an exiled child
the home you dream of living in, one day

hands follow the wire
pressing out shapes the heart
wants.

CHRONICLES OF HORSE

The town is full of drumming
of invisible horses' hooves
get ready
even the snail is running

banners straighten in the breeze
on altars of the chosen churches
sit blessed lottery balls
horses are coming

we know what is expected
we know what we must do
in drench of utmost sweat

we're drumming, running, racing
we're messengers of gods
we're gods, we're glory chasing—

****

We pray to our ancestor the ass
we shoulder nativity's blessing
the night-cool church above us
soothes us with peace divine
stars and saints at rest
help spirit collocate equine.

None of us are losers.

******

You can't go anywhere without us
we carry you, good and ill
across valley and hill
white dappled black
grey chestnut dun

spotted and streaked
and our marks of pastern, fetlock, coronet and sock
snip and stripe, blaze and star
these are not the words we use among ourselves
but we let them pass

****

According to the artists we are always there
drowning when the Red Sea parts
bearing heavy soldiers to yet another crucifixion
witnessing the slaughter of innocents
we bite and kick each other sometimes
but no horse murders another

****

The Bay Horse who will carry St Augustine from Rome
smiles at his pious burden
we will trot along just fine
I will pick out a way upon your stony path

The Bay Horse who has delivered St Augustine to Milan
has a very well-muscled chest
and a slight frown
as if someone is missing.

****

At the end we will be there
when the trumpet sounds
the dead rise incorruptible
you will be changed
we stay as we are
Flood, Fire, Famine, Death

****

In town we're privy to the gossip
we bring in headlines, hearsay, scoops
we jingle in with ducats
whose exact weight we can tell
likewise linen spices building materials
according to our grade
we smell of leather

we have got used to working together
origins and rank dissolve in sweat
we can't escape
we're shackled, hobbled, shod with steel
and anyway where could we go?

****

One day some man will cut our throats
chop us up and throw us to the dogs
we hope it is the ones who run beside us
at least they'll honour us with gratitude.

****

Paint tells terrible lies.
When did you ever see the clouds of flies that torment us?
But sometimes we glimpse ecstasy
in the cool of the evening we drink from clear, still pools
beauty in the beholder's eye, of course
long-lashed, rich brown
now praise our velvet grace and majesty of bone.

****

Wartime. Again. Forged spears
and swords. Thin coverings.
We trudge to whichever bloody field will be our grave.
We are expendable. Horsemeat.

I have my own scars. New wounds
Are on their way. It is not equitable.
It never is.

****

Did you ever come hunting with us?
Deep in the woods
flitting shadows on our flanks
like phantom deer

to hold your nerve before a wild boar's jabbing tusks
is good for boasts while dogs and hunters feast.

****

When we came out of the forest
there was One who stayed behind
She—we think it was a She—
grew a sword in case of need
and to point the way.
There are certain humans who can understand this
and to whom she appears in dreams.

Nubs of wings fret shoulder-blade and haunch
our masters just see saddle sores.

****

Frescoes never show us mating
or making love
we can show humans a thing or two
they say they can prick up their ears
but they can't.

****

There are a couple of saints who particularly require our presence
St George, who couldn't kill a dragon
unless he had advantage from our height
St Martin, who needs to look down
upon the beggar he then decides to half-clothe.
Neither ever thanked their horse.

We detest St Eligius who forced a reluctant horse to be shod
And St Anne the patron of those who ride and whip us.
We debate the merits of various holy women who were denied
    mounts
and we remark that while their hell has no horses
neither does their heaven.

****

After rain, rain, rain, rain
here's an ark, finally
get in before the heavens open again
says Noah who has made us all half deaf with his hammering

the leopards don't trust him
the camels get claustrophobic
the dragons haven't shown up
that's the end of them then
they were a fire hazard.

All eyes are on us
very well then as usual we will lead the way
fall in behind
follow

****

My portrait is found all over this city
at the court and town hall
in every souvenir shop
I carry a field marshal out of camp

caparisoned charger draped in gold
most richly dressed White Horse
black-diamonded
inscrutable

Everyone knows the commander's name
turncoat restored, victorious in this castle siege
what am I doing here?
It's so desolate there's not a single blade of grass
is there to be a parley?

The loneliest horse in the universe
knows humans like to kill.

With thanks to Simone Martini, Pinturicchio, Bartolo di Fredi, Lippo Memmi, Benozzo Gozzoli and other artists, principally in Siena where the Palio race is run every year in the town square, and in honour of all quattrocento horses.

CLOUDS

Veil of unsayable
clouds scudding past
in silver and grey

mask to the moon's masquerade cloak
they pause to tease
then drift, immaterial

lumpily between us
and sunrise, clouds
are sky clods

our stratospheric aspirations
materialise in clouds
sky writing, cuneiform

loose, precise, mutable
hulked, combed free
life's changeable as clouds.

CONVERSATION BETWEEN THE DOG AND I

I wish you could tell me if you think the chicken's off
your nose, big nose, a hundred times more sensitive
than mine, evolution afterthought anyway
knows, I'm sure, the difference

it's an expensive business which is a stretch but that's my glad
    promise
so we'll stick to the bargain of what Co-op says is cut-price
it's just that in these times of waste's alarms
the sorry business of scraping your dinner into the compost bin

raises questions of who can afford what and why
I don't have answers to inequity
and I still have the washing up to do so I would be glad

if something at least as good as gristle nourished you
and if there was not philosophy as well to have to chew.

DOVER BEACH

Scrunch of pebbles had its poem
hush of waves, its shush

night filled the bay with longing
lights blinked from far away

over black water sound carried fast and clear
spinning out the mystery

why two people sat at a window
intimates, looking out.

DRAGONFLY

Soft-bellied on moss
air unveiled
feeling the power of the sun

kitted up in biker gloves and helmet
seemingly motionless
but revving up, heat-ready

wings biplane strong
pearlescent
cloud-veined

will whirr, dart and hover
power show-off skywards
life on the edge of gone.

DREAM OF FLYING

This is your pilot speaking
it's a bit late to wonder about training or professionalism
or even phoney accents

you can of course be the awkward customer
who has an urgent need for the toilet
just as the seat-belt sign goes on

or you can let your ideas of upfront
go vague, and accept
take-off, safety, in my hands.

EVERYWHERE HOMES ARE IN CHAINS

Homeland security
home and away
homing pigeon
Home Office
living at home
working from home
home team, home side
home insurance, because your home is at risk
home help

unhomed, rehomed, homeless
homesick
home thoughts from abroad
posted home
starter home, second home
at home to Your Lordship
Home Counties, Home Guard

leaving home
home town, home address
phone home, E.T.
home cooking
home stretch, romp home
care home
which used to be called old people's home
home truths

homebody, home-maker
the homely in looks
spiritual home, if you believe in that
sent home from school
the road home
home delivery
home furnishings
in the privacy of your own home
homestead, homeowner, voter

home waters, for dolphins and warships
home sweet home
home entertainment system
viewers at home may wish to look away now

home screen, home page, hashtag #home
send them home
back where they came from

the camp is home to
the field is home to
the world is home to

we are far from home
dreaming of home
homeward bound.

GOING TO THE FESTIVAL: A DIARY

Airport
Two loved-up Sikhs in matching turbans
are on the hunt
for breakfast

the barista who is two hours into a red-eye shift
manages a smile which seems genuine
that's more an art than frothed design

here almost all the world is skybound
and few are tied to earth

everyone wears canvas shoes or trainers
with low-cut socks
I hope for winged sandals but there aren't any
my neighbour's painted toes are salmon, overcooked

the muscled father of two small and pretty girls
holds Saudi passports, green with a gold palm tree
dates matter when you travel

a man with anxious wife
scoots by on a contraption
which protects his plastered leg
his teenage son sulks
suffering the shame of uncool parents

today I want to be generous
I admire beads, beards, dresses, plaits
I watch an international blonde
glide by in fresh-pressed linen
does she iron her clothes herself?

the queue is interminably slow
we edge forward, voluntary prisoners

to board planes, gull-white
snub-nosed, sleek as sharks
air, water, either's fine for those about to step off earth
to climb the stairs into a whale belly
dry, deodorised
my seat's a window throne
from where
      flying godlike above water
chequerboard fields and fleecy clouds
I fall asleep and dream of gardens

Arrival Hall
Do you spick English?
sorry I squeak your language
I make fearful ragged sounds, owlchick
where do I find the train station
strain translation
where is the protection of poetry?

Station
I have cracked the code I am Bletchley's finest
a ticket drops out
we glide away
finches on the wing examine
which chenille field to glean

Walk
The first thing to do is slip the tether
explore the obvious
all too soon this new will turn into familiar
against that frisson is humidity
a fork of lightning dances round the tower
the swifts lower their game

nearby, in padlocked chapel
Madonna of the Snows envisions winter
I am Master of the Guide Book
two pigeons wish to share my lunch

faith, charity
crumbs.

Medieval Vertigo
I am above the swifts
terracotta tiles clatter in chromatic tints
they're not the only secret

moss lives up here, strategic
only soldiers and angels see it

Zoological Museum
I suppose it had to be done.
Mercury in the Veins
A Severed Leg, Human
Ribcage Boned Like A Chicken

black hand stiffened in a final curl
blood's circulation
mimicked in silver
pauper's grave for the other bits of him?

And while we're asking, how do you take in
all these dead birds, faded, stuffed
a parliament of fowls most artfully arranged
hooks, crooks and spoonbills, beaks and claws
trophied behind glass?
What did we learn besides their names?
Our power to kill?

Together
Their haircuts rhyme
their glasses chime
their striped shirts harmonize
they're tousled, tanned
they understand
how hand in hand
is sometimes best served by sitting slightly apart.

The Breakfast Club of Poets
They greet, they laugh, they sit, they photograph
they seem so glamorous
here's one: coiffed hair, red jacket, white silk blouse
white jeans with print of roses, sandalled heels
red leather bag, gold chains
and very stylish sunglasses
I have just broken mine
I feel naked

Hello to June, he says
the light's longueurs are softest now
his audience is holding up their cameraphones
gesture of offerings, high praise

Amore
When I am far from home
I love to hear
that love lives everywhere
that wit and sexiness criss-cross the air
of all old cities
we speak a common tongue
saltimbocca

yet I miss you
like I miss the letter y.

At the Festival
How long did it take her to put on
these multiple adornments?
Six silver rings
two silver bracelets
one heavy, one serpentine
beaded wrist cuff
silver earrings (dangling participles)
silver collar
beaded ankle cuff
two toe rings?

With all these shavings of the moon
she walks in weighty silver
so metalled that she chinks and clinks
I would rather listen to it than to this poetry

Translator
At the word *dwarf* she pauses
head on one side, smiling
wonders aloud if it is boy or girl
conjectural gender

the thought, she says, conjecturally
seems likeliest to be
to belong, to be said
by a woman.

Park
In a park where long grass plots to bury picnic tables
and termite installations form a biennale
a dice-rolled six of old folk are playing cards
each knows the strength and weakness of the others
how luck is dealt with each fresh draw

adjacent, teenagers revising
laptops earplugs headphones smartphones
isolated concentration

Mobilising
Morning. I shower off
intensities of dreams and double up
espresso.
Shops unshutter.
Some sweep their steps and stoops
under the shade of trees whose names I do not know.

The bus station sees stops and starts of journeys.
The trees wave handkerchiefs of green: time to go.

GOLD CUP

Cheltenham

Along the gallops of downland
race thundering horses
curve of the chalk is horseshoe, sweaty

along the road roll five tipsy Irishmen
down for the races and staying drunk
their bowler hats accurately tipping

lifted to say top of the morning
to you missus
may the wind bless your horse

a tenner each way, odds on
or long shot, outsider unranked
you hold the name close

closer than colours you memorized
heraldry's cryptograms
the divinations last longer than the race

with libation to wash down the rain
whet your whistle
breath and foam in many clouds

along the oval track jockeys
urge on their tiring horses
luck and skill, fate and weather, photo-finish will decide.

GOYA'S DOG

In the Ermita San Antonio de la Florida, a chapel in Madrid with frescoes by Goya, there is a circular scene around the cupola which shows St Antony raising a man back to life in order to answer the question: who murdered him? The saint's father has been accused; the corpse says he was not the murderer —but does not say who was. A crowd watches: in contemporary dress, all sorts of characters look on, in all sorts of attitudes. Among the figures is a hunchback with a beautiful dog, a brown hound, who leans forward towards the saint with more attention than many of the people.

I've seen that dog, loping beside its brute master
a she, I think, born affectionate and curious
quizzical about the human world
given to sniffing the hems of robes
friar, woman, beggar

her keeper, who will never have a woman
unless he kidnaps one
loves this dog so much
he will go hungry to let her feed
first pick of scraps
last bite of crust

she's silky-eared, a *maja*, chocolate velvet
a beauty he can only glimpse lopsidely
all handsome, as he with hunch and broken grin will never be
all ears, to hear this saint

the keeper thinks the saint is smart
he's on to something, surely
charging to raise the dead
you'd never run out of customers

the dog has heard something different
under a smell of piety, a hunger for the truth
urgency of question
moral emergency

playful, obedient, meek and sad
her eyes are soulful
can a dog go to heaven by being good
she wonders, stretching the question
in long arched neck, flat ears

and listening to the saint
she wonders why
in this beautiful world
truth is in short supply.

Note: close-up photographs reveal the dark shape is human shoulder, back and body. That it looks exactly like a hound from below is an optical illusion: deliberate, by a dog-loving artist?

GRENFELL TOWER

St Maximos the hut burner
hated attachment
when his hut got too homely
he burnt it

and moved on
no sin to delight in a new home
arrested development, maybe, commitment-phobe
but forward-looking

if by accident your home catches fire
burns down
your heart is a hearth of ashes

there is no phoenix, no dove
only crows.

HOME AGAIN, AGAIN §

Brushing a scented and potbound geranium
I pause at the door, key in hand
home is knowing which key will fit
and whether to turn it right or left

a pile of post splatters the carpet
leaking the secret
you live here
and someone has sent you a parcel which could not be
delivered

I am responsible for everything
material wrappings, mysterious purpose
in cold syllables of foreign language
the house whispers retreat

when the kettle is on and the boiler settles
it comes back to me, uncertainty, certainty
this is home, home, home
scented geranium, potbound.

HOMELESS §

There's an Ancient Mariner on the High Street
he says he's homeless, doesn't drink, doesn't smoke
and he really is homeless unlike some of the guys
who pitch up and beg

tatterdemalion, filthy fingernails
his nose broken more than once by the squashed look of it
or maybe he smashed to the ground
in stupor of drink or whatever thin-cut drugs he could smoke

I'm a long way from home, he says
his accent is Australian
I can't get benefits
and I've got a daughter who needs better than being out on the
        streets
she's autistic—you know what autistic is?

Yes, and how old is your daughter?
Eighteen and we can pass for a couple
so the hostel rate is cheaper
it's cheaper still if you pay for three nights
… he rattles off sums, sticks hands in holed pockets
produces a fiver and some shiny coins
look! I just need this much
then I can go to the agencies
use their phones and computers
get benefits sorted

thank you, he says, for not turning away
for a kind look

we dig deep
so much for taxes, two lots
'tis the season
and no girl should be bedding down with her father
we also tell him of church shelters

oh bless you, he says, and look!
I've almost enough for three nights now
and he piles the money in our hands
look! Who else would do that, says he

when we hand it back and bid him good luck and farewell
fare better
he disappears flash down an alley

why should it matter
whether he told the truth or not?

IMPEDIMENTS TO GRACE

Impediments to grace arise, arthritic
time's running out
we limp

blinking light will stop us in our tracks
conversions sharp as prickly pears
give time its crimp

there's no return to small hand safe in large hand
it's hand in glove with liability
our spoke-holes glimped

in glimpse of undecidability
a prickled pairing graces hand in hand
limping, we run ahead.

LECHLADE TO TADPOLE BRIDGE

for Nicola Watson, with gratitude

Acres of dandelion clocks
tell fractional atomic difference
between each light-headed moment

timepiece puffs its metaphysical fluff
here passing gone
in field's expanse they stretch away to pointilliste horizon

we are moving dots ... satnav plotting between points
old locks and weathered trees
escapees

hatchlings make the grasses quiver
clucks of alarm from mother bird
cry gather, shelter in her circle

stone bastions jut
abut the bank
strutted, braced, shuttered

concrete mushrooms, they hold
a sagging trace of boredom
the loopholed hours of conscripts

they might be ancient temples, mithraic remnants
except the blockhead thought survives
will the enemy come, will the enemy ever come

all these things press singly
then make a daisy-chain of histories
seasonally

the summer version's full of blossom
cow-parsley, buttercups, a hawthorn edge tumbling
with path of froth

mayflies hit new points in air
where they leap daringly
azimuth, zenith, apogee

swans navigate domestic reach of river
a weir their boundary and the stubborn weed
needing to be shovelled through

upending, question-marking where?
aquatic forage turns out more profitable
than dabbling

yet there's little of narrative, merely
small movements, restless moving on
of dragonfly among the reeds and brambles

call of hidden cuckoo
chugging pleasure boat's returning chug
curlew unreproved, unbeached, cries back.

LEPER FIELD, DEVON

The sun in winter never touches
the north side of this field
here stones were harsh and harrows broke

first it was lumps, then more lumps
sickening foreboding
undodgeable as death

their names went warty
whole families fell silent
pilgrim figures walked downstream

would you know when you broke bread
fresh, crusty
if its flour had passed through a leper's hand?

LILY

Lily, who is
in her infinity
the ghost made present
of all we might have wished for

there is no reproach
only sympathy
in this quality doth the Lily excel

Lily, who
is in her infinity
the guest made present
of solitude's conviviality

there is no idle chat
only telepathy
in this quality doth the Lily excel.

LONG-LEGGED FLOWER BEETLE

Oedemera nobilis

She walks in blue-green armoured beauty
sleek long slim body
emerald wing-cased

only the male has jewel pouches
which only the female can size up
with her connoisseur's eye
appreciatively

it lies in a flower, buttercup, dog-rose
purposefully, taking pollen
as it fancies, not for hive mind

delicate antennae twitch
body-length probes
sunbather reading a book

legs geometrically arranged
fibonacci, probably, in jasper black
body low to the ground, pollenhound
steady in the breeze of swaying flower

uppermost is green jewelled body
in soirée greens
in which it gads about in daylight
purring flowery anecdotes

and yet so simple: beetle
wings, jewels, flower, flight.

LOVE THY NEIGHBOUR

Daggers drawn paled to contempt
which rested there, a barrier
then over the fence
curled a tendril

pink jasmine
the kind she liked least
but looking at it
shears suspended

she thought she could learn to live with it.

MAIN ENGINE CUT OFF

MECO cards are written by astronauts before launch, and sent by Ground Control when—and if—the launch is successful.

I.

Dear World if you read this
you will know
all has gone according to plan
you rise in my view
blue marbled with green and white.

Of course this doesn't mean
I'll make it back
but we'll know
after centuries of wondering
what it is like on the moon.

II.

Dear World if you read this
you will know
our plans proved ineffectual
useless, wildly misplaced
you rise in my view
scorched, bleached, denuded.

Of course this doesn't mean
we will come back
but we will know
after decades of not wondering enough
what it is like to lose our home.

OAKS

Torrington, Devon—a Royalist stronghold in the Civil War

There's a gall wasp who gives oaks
arthritic fingers clutching at air
they gnarl and knot

filling the valley mist spreads
from the river where otter prints
incise the mud with hope of survival

what's left, tattered and broadcast
musters a wild place, olden times
cavalier oaks surviving their pests.

NOW IT'S MAGNOLIAS

Before midnight most nights
witching hour
clink clink clink
empties in dustbin
vermouth with the curate
playing scrabble till the clock
struck its familiar anagram

in those days we had facing windows
kitchen sink serial
hallo all good take care goodbye
semaphore of waving hands
the more natural as she became deaf
and our windows grew longer acquainted

she had lovage, I had sage
we shared euphorbia and a rambling rose
sunlight lit my garden slantwise from hers
through the loosest of wire fences
we swapped apples
my eaters for her cookers
which she coddled in newspaper and stored in her cellar

when she aged and found it a struggle
I cut her grass, weeded and pruned
as best I could, knowing of old
there was always something choice in flower
speckled astrantia, yellow peony, barrenwort
I coaxed them under the fence
and her optimism took root
it's always a good year for something, she'd say.

Now it's magnolias.

ODORATA

The catalogue said they'd be singles and bicolour
fragrant, old-fashioned

it did not say the scent is so heady
it knocks you sideways
the littlest hoverflies hesitate
before approaching

it did not say, the colours test credulity
sugared almond, lilac, pink
sheet white, blood red, insistent
blue reverie
mauve and cerise like rival bishops

it did not say, few painters attempt them
nor how in a pale green jug
they catch any heart
that knows longing or loss.

ORB WEAVERS

Tall lilies in pots
I am expecting a Madonna

inspecting the lilies I see
a spider at every other juncture
nubbed in a leaf joint
they are resident

Mrs Pied à Terre
Mrs Piano Nobile
Mrs Crashing on Sofa
Mrs Attic

they live in a skyscraper, green
with late summer
silvered with webs
they spin elegies

dessicated cricket, wrapped feast
moulders a leaf-umbrella
sheltering an ancestor, dead, dried
shifting in the breeze

perhaps Mrs Piano Nobile
knows arachnid last rites
perhaps Mrs Attic
admires her garden panorama

bending one knee, any angel
lighting here with many-coloured wings
would see tall lilies in clay pots
and residents confused by visitation.

PATAGONIA

Some Patagonia of the mind
is ringed by mountains
so grand there surely lies beyond
a land of homage

what passes for sublime
is furry kin to hangover and flu
dizzy recognition of excess
that floats, in vanity, below the view

it's territory of puma, thin, white-ribbed
of pangolin in rusty armour
of birds in frantic emerald clamour
and vermin in dead forests cribbed

it has its charms though
its ocean storms beat back invaders
its clouds disguise, its rains chastise
and I can go there without you.

POLICHINELLE PAINTINGS BY ALFRED COHEN

'Pulcinella, a man without dignity, is nevertheless indispensable to us all' –
Antonio Fava, *mask maker and master of commedia dell'arte.*

Reds all day. Tomato. Fire engine.
Cadmium rages. Tabasco.
Fury. Naphthol red, slashing

Blood comes in scarlet, crimson, madder.
Alfa Romeo, revving at a red light
impatient to get to gloss lips

But something's happened
a punch in the guts
from losing

I'll cudgel your brains.
Chilli fierce.
Boil. Burn. Seethe.

Then I'll just dangle a smile
Beak, belly, codpiece.
Your blue-eyed boy again.

RECIPROCALS

Breathless as if sobbing you leave me a message
will you remind me to give you a cable of lights
at the end of an evening we have not yet begun

sobbing as if breathless I give you a message
will you remind me to tell you
you are a cable of lights
at the end of an evening we need to re-run.

RECOGNITION

Time is the colour of bamboo
lattice around this screen

it's not my heirloom
but I feel a kinship with it

the blossom is first froth of thorn
the birds are plentiful and squat

an artist thought it fit to paint
dirt-dusted flowers and squabbling sparrows

lowly, lovely
understood.

RESCAFFOLDING §

Slant of black rain
italic sleet
morse code
underscore, dash

Elegant in suspension we find a chair
circling its own thoughts
weightless, burdened
unseated in free fall

We have seats in the thick of it
ringside circus, shackle
pole slotted into pole
so there is somewhere safe to climb into

What does a sequence express
that is not straight out in single?
I contemplate new constellations
in joined-up writing

You shoulder stakes, hoping for links
to make something of
rods, poles, perches
iron measures of grace.

SCAFFOLDING: A CRASH COURSE §

Good foundations are essential
for soft or doubtful surfaces, use sole boards
on uneven ground, cut steps for base plates
for heaviest duty, use concrete baulks
add guard rails and stop boards
you must think about safety, safety first

basejack, standard, ledger, transom
batten, coupler, ties and brackets
hoop irons stamped with makers' names
tubes and boards
grip, fasten, lock

steady on
there are three types of coupler
right angle, putlog and swivel
right angle couplers join ledgers or transoms to standards
putlog or single couplers join transoms to ledgers
spacings are standard, usually
a width of four boards
to join tubes, use sleeve couplers
or end to end joint pins
also called spigots
a façade brace will limit sway at every level

there is minimum overhang, a handspan
there is maximum overhang, a ratio
no more than four times the thickness of the board

or you can lash light poles of bamboo
with coconut rope
and have done.
Think of this emblematically, practically
scaffolds are rarely independent structures

you need to tie in at regular intervals
put-through ties are put through structure openings
such as windows
ensure a solid fit by packing timber wedges

there are box ties, anchor ties, lip ties
reveal ties are not well regarded
if ties can't be used safely
always you think about safety
make rakers from triangles back to the base
use pump jack and ladder jack
swing stages, crawling boards.

Ready to use
here come mason, bricklayer, tiler
plasterer, decorator
foreman and boss.

SHADOW PLAY AT HOME §

My double got up today
and got things done
finally cleaned that mouldy window
made cakes, wrote a masterpiece
learnt the thrush's song
and how to ride bareback

my double can move mountains
lower sea levels, find other planets
get rid of tyrants in a finger snap
trouble is, my double is a shadow
who bubbles up
deferring doing

SITTING OPPOSITE

on a train to the West Country

An elderly man shouts into his phone
he is calling a friend
who must make sure
that Somerset County Council should buy a copy
of the new Debretts
there's a special offer
fifty pounds off
so it's only four hundred

Why does he think the citizens of Somerset
need a Debretts?
Is he in it? Does he want to look himself up
author of his being?

Duke of Somerset, an extinct line
not even a burgundy butterfly
is he arch-royalist, cavalier
with taxpayers' money?
Does he Lord it over his fellows
in the snug of a London club
or a Cotswold-stone hotel?

He is insistent. They must
Buy a copy. Will she see it is done?
What poor woman does his bidding
or makes up excuses?
He has the loudness of gone-deaf
his clothes are lived-in, heirloomed
he is bony, harsh
one to whom the peerage and baronetage
are precious

he stands up for his principled phone call
the train emptied at the last stop
he is King of the Carriage
and I, entitled bourgeois, am sitting opposite.

SMALL CONSOLATION

Across town a phone rang
funeral news, and weeping

chequered existences
ghosts and shades

chalk paths tilt downland upward
serpentine ladders

footsteps echo the dead
and so you mourn, sob, live.

SOUNDSCAPE OF HOME §

The neighbours are away
thank god for that
the mother always yelling at the child
who has learned to yell back

in pursuit of instilling manners she is mannerless
and so the child bangs, thumps, stomps up and down

you wait for the other shoe to fall
but for once it is quiet and still

bricks breathe again, relaxed
space expands, attentive
galactic depths reappear
resonance is palpable

the deerhound and I wander out to the garden to look at stars
we stand together close, wordless
mute with wonder at the night

then he barks at the clouds and I rebuke him
far too loudly.

SUITCASE

Old age thinks of life's span
what was it all for
all that striving and loving and saying

Georgian carriageway shrinks
to a packhorse bridge
where were you going that you came this way

yet somehow here is today
which continues an everyday
which grows in a compost of yesterdays

yesteryears now: we talk of them
feeling them farther away but simplified
forgetfulness can be a mercy

I want to go when I'm ready, you say
and not linger
your suitcase is packed

porter, carer, daughter
human in kindness, well meant
all hear confessions

torn ankle, swollen knee
today another broken tooth
you're tissue-paper light.

SURVEILLANCE

My droids are panicky tonight
like sheep who've sensed a predator
or how I imagine sheep were

after the Deluge we were all rewired
luminous glow fell in patches
like mist, or how I remember mist was

every now and again I wish for a life
free to be silly, like lambs
cyber unfenced.

SWIMMER

for Jo Croft—swimmer, artist, writer

In ripples of dark comes a flame
from a lighthouse
dancing on black water

this is the way
follow me

coasts give certainty as waves
rush freedom on you
then take it away

you know how to resist
how to surrender, persist, make headway
out to sea

all that could be flows into now
storms and harbours buoy you up.

TERRITORIALITY

When summer night draw in
it seems a sin
to stay indoors

but island inland chill
hangs cold outdoors in frills
so it is not I who goes

into the garden, where blackbird alarm
dices a corner of the air
where moths flutter along evening closing up for the night

where roses tumble and an apple tree
twists one limb
above wildflowers, its tiny orchard plot.

THAT THING YOU DO BEFORE YOU DO
THE NEXT THING

Somewhere between being chained to my desk
and at a loose end
I dial up indulgence

tell personnel I am on a training course
for the next life
confetti on departing bus

there are moths who pass on codes in urban gardens
caged birds who sing of freedom best
there are slugs who get there in the end

unquantifiable to human resources
comes loosening
taut soul stretching, gratified.

TOO LATE

When the ship left early without me
rats on the quayside jeered
as the boat grew small in the distance
even the seagulls sneered

I felt a sickening feeling
a pounding tearing heart
a sense of self went reeling

my future fell apart

at the jagged edge of catastrophe
cruelty's punch of fate
hit hopes with a staggering blow
in those bitterest words: too late.

TWO UP, TWO DOWN §

Two tiny figures perch precariously
within their stilted world

each of their exquisite balancing acts
is managed, stage-managed

lines walk past us to old thresholds
edge of the forest, edge of the plain

left hanging, possibilities are hammered
into ladders nonchalantly leaning

the tiny figures command important things
chair, staircase, refuge, trap.

VOICE

It's hard to hear your shape of voice
uppermost perhaps in letters
rattling, understated, droll

it ages as your walk does
unsteadied by illness
unbalanced by loss

timbre which is music scaffolded by words
pattern of resistances and surge
voice rarely talks of itself.

UNLOADING

Tell the one I love of love
unburdened in the dark
a tall ship
from which we disembark.

WALK ON THE BEACH

Westward Ho!, North Devon

for my sister

The tide is out on this long sandy beach
so the waves are far off and small
white curls, catching the sun
in a rhyme with a seagull who glides
high over us as if to see
what the fuss is about

the sands have pools of pale blue
an artist has come and gone with madness
of watercolour, obsessive sky blue
to outdo the dogs who run around
shapeshifting, white like the waves
black like the rocks, sandy as sand

they bark with joy at so much air
salty and fresh
they bark with joy at the light
clean and precise
they bark with joy at joy
to be out and free

they chase balls as if they are in love
while the light smiles and falls on us all
equally blessing
as if the cars parked up behind the shingle
would never hold captives
or say it is time to go home.

WEATHER DIARIST

Port Meadow

Frost, dusting bramble and silvering twigs.
Cockleshell clouds.
Light spilling onto water, spreading.
Water doubling light.

The big trees wrap skirts of warmth
Around young trees, who bow or curtsey.
Daisies turn up pale faces.

Reflections—willow, hawthorn—
Exact in single plane as spider webs
Hung out in hope of random gnats.

Dogs, walkers, runners
Young women rowing fast and strong
Rowlock thud
And splash, diminishing.

Calm. Set Fair. Glove weather.
Heart tranquil. Storm allayed.

WILLIAM COPWER'S SHAVING MIRROR

at the Cowper and Newton Museum, Olney

It is morning and the poet
still in white nightshirt
is shaving

at his washstand, a mirror
catches his bedroom
backwards

adding a sliver of town
all-night drunks stumbling
out of the Red Lion

the poet's face is long and bony
wide mouth, soft eyes are sensitive
his faculties are god-given

every day, scrape away
sin
a mirror within

every morning he looks in his shaving mirror
to perceive himself
as cheek and chin

no mark of sin
upon cheek and chin
upon throat his hand trembles slightly

percussive birdsong merely
blackbird hymn
praising the God of Light and upper lip

he dips his blade in cold water
his skin stiffens
his nightshirt is thin

whinny of horses beyond
clatter of pattens below
rustle of leaves, spit-splat of rain

every morning
new promise, good faith
benediction of cheek and chin

every morning this mirror frames his face
his face fills this mirror
innocent

his hands are clean
our Redeemer's blood
all washed away

leaving love
of God
of shaven cheek and chin.

WOBBEGONG

O wobbegong, whose aboriginal name
describes your shaggy beard
you've disappeared
almost
into the sand

where you lie, immobile
almost sessile
moss starts to grow on you like sloth
slow moving, not moving, unmoving

you are a paisley shawl slung on a reef
patterned like you
two white dots pretend to be eyes
above your fixed gaze
your tail can bob like a lure
if you can be bothered
which seems unlikely

your lobed ornaments criss-cross
channels in delta, sacred ideograms, carpet's knotted fringe
tasselled wobbegong, lace in place
inscribes a breathing space.